# BREAKING

Roshan James

OTHER TITLES

This Is My Story, This Is My Song

2017

Art of the Unknown

2018

# TABLE OF CONTENTS

# A SONG OF TRIBUTE

Exploring the ever elusive

In a sea of aching sameness


This is our reclamation

And holding

Of what we have been told we are not


A search for peace

In the wreckage of belief


Learning to keep

Harmony within

## PROLOGUE

Living and whole feeling

Yet incomplete

We are She

Who planted

Beautiful Life

In cracked soil

Breaking

# BRITTLE

Breaking


Fluorescent buzz

Feeds at the fringes of focus

It is cold and frenetic

And we are the bone finger branches

Wrapped in an old cardigan

Sitting

Outside the sick rooms

Where all of us find ourselves

From time to time

Sometimes inside, sometimes

Outside the places where the floors are

Washed twice daily

But nothing ever feels clean or fixed

Breaking


We run red lights

From exhaustion


Maybe we'll get there

Breaking


Perhaps, you thought it was

You

As they said good-bye

(Or when they didn't say anything at all)


It was part of themselves

They couldn't face

Breaking

Scarred bark curling

Over bare-knuckled boughs

Withering

After our lively start

At the loss of lifeblood in our veins

We wonder if we will ever bear leaves

Again

If we will ever take in the sun and

Transform the light

In our closed fists

Breaking



Insecurity has a way of slipping from

Our tongues

As frost covers late autumn grass that

Still smells like summer

As a barn on fire

And the horses

Run loose

There is no repairing

What burns


It will burn

It will release

Breaking


We are brittle before we break

After our thick-skinned hiding

Thins out, hardens


Before the hardening starts to fissure


We are brittle on the surface

And through the cracks

Our softness seeps

Cracking cold,

Sharp snaps

Echo into our bones

Breaking


I turned my temple

Upside

Down

Searching for the cup of life

For a drop from the well

For a word from a stranger

Breaking


It took awhile

The water ran so long

Wearing down to the stone

A bed

Of granite forged

And strewn

River rock

It was cold and brisk

And the rock was slippery for standing

As I took the first few steps in


That freedom was always ours

Breaking


Our first disappointment has a way of

Filling our lungs

While everyone watches

To see

How heavy a heart can feel

Breaking


We all have ugly moments
Tired weeks
Scars so jagged they criss-cross
Down our backs
Tightening around our waists
Then moving snake-like ahead
Like they know the way
Pulling us
Into a ragged-breath run
Away from the mark-makers
While the lead balloons tied
To our swollen ankles
Add weight
They thud and drag
Trailing
Reminders of how
One step can feel like regret

Breaking


I didn't know
What my hip bones felt like
Against my palms
Until my jeans needed a wiggle
And you offered me baggy clothes
And told me to straighten up


Or what it felt like to crave
Then hate my own skin
For wanting


Or to be self-deprived
To the level of self-loathing


Or that all of this would whisper
At the edges of my day
For so long

Breaking


How long is it our duty,

And honourably so,

To carry other peoples'

Shame

As our own?

# WHEN THE AIR LEAVES
# THE ROOM

Breaking

And this is how I learned

Soft things still try

To be strong

Breaking


In the high-ceilinged holy places

Where colourful glass tells old stories

It is dark and quiet

And in the sepulchre

There is a shiver of afterlight

Breaking

We may as well be standing

With the ghosts in the walls

Looking

Into the rooms

We used to walk

Breaking


After

Feels baggy

Like a fitted sheet

Come loose

At the corner

Breaking

Where can we sleep

When bullets find us

In our beds?

Breaking


Mother, I know
your night pains


The silent
Scream
Under your skin
Splitting tissue and bone and breath


We are the ones who fight with
Ourselves
To keep the peace

Breaking


How do we pray

When we can't breathe?

Breaking

'I'm in here,'

she points to her chest


They look, but can't see

Breaking


'I'm in here,'

trying not to put my fist

through my own walls


Dramatic, they say

Aggressive, they say

Calm down, they say


I'll just stay in here

Breaking

'I'm in here,'

but you can't see me,

you can only see my smile

Breaking

'I'm in here,'

she hugs herself,

holding her breath

Breaking

They are with me in the mirror

All around the edges

Elbowing each other

For gawking views

Meeting me every morning

Ready with their careful questioning

*Really Concerned*

With their maybes and should'ves

And this might be why

It's feeling a little crowded in here

These days

Breaking


We are

What fills

The emptiness

We are

Breaking


In the still life

Of thin evening light

Dust motes

Turn lazy

Hanging mid air


Breathe in, breathe out

Everything dances

Around us again

# LIFTING

Breaking


It's not the strong voice

But the quiver

In the throat

That calls

The Spirit

Breaking


If we listen

To our bodies

We will know

How to heal

Breaking


It all comes out at night

This wanting

To be on good terms with the world

Breaking

Destroy

Knowing

I can make whole

What you believe

Breaking

Over the void

We call out

For reunion

Breaking

All the ways

In which we

Open

And call ourselves

Home

Breaking

Requires
Being
Before

Creating
Requires
Being

Before
Creating
Requires
Being

Breaking

Hearing the footsteps

Of the river

Wading

Through the forest


I can see a softly round form

Between

Branches


Reaching for the moon

# RISING

Breaking


Laughter

Peals

Over the brim

Breaking


Spirit to Spirit

May we speak


Spirit to Spirit

May we hear

Breaking

Ever-beings

Wildling things

Of the sweetest

Good

Breaking

Expanding grace

Reaches

The ears of the unclaimed

Breaking

Room

In

Which

To

Spread

Out

Breaking


Unfurling

Palm,

Redemption

Begins in the Spirit

Breaking


Light in a dappled yellow dance

Over the long-cut green

Hope always lingers

In the morning air

Breaking

How intimate

To care

Breaking

Scoop out the remnants

And kiss them away

To the wind


Strength and grace

Strength and grace

Strength and grace


Pulsing

Through our veins

Breaking


Bright the blood

In our cheeks

It is brave passage

Breaking

Still

And yet

In constant

Quiver

Breaking


Breath

Is our artistry

Breaking

There is nothing more

to pursue

In balance

Breaking


I will shake loose

From my smouldering core

To show you

How mere emotion

Can thunder

Breaking

The radical

And the disobedient

Have set us free

Breaking

All are worthy

All are vessels

All are breaking

All are light

All our Spirit

All are free

Breaking

Call it balance or completion

Parts of the whole reuniting


We dance with the Unknown


We dance with ourselves

Breaking


What is Good

Sees its reflection

In us

Breaking


Through the sun
Catching
On my eyelashes
She
Is
Pris
med
Light


Rising and falling and rising


And my heart follows
Into the swell

Breaking

Always flowing in being,

Our energy is ever-changing

Where we stand,

All around us,

And so,

It's no wonder

We don't always

Feel certain

And sometimes

We forget

How powerful we are

We are mountains in motion

Breaking


She is

Without

Edges

Breaking

Heart centre

Is home

Breaking

There is

Endlessness

In us

Breaking